KOREAN FOLK SONGS

STARS IN THE SKY AND DREAMS IN OUR HEARTS

ROBERT SANG-UNG CHOI

illustrations by SAMEE BACK

TUTTLE Publishing

Tokyo | Rutland, Vermont | Singapore

Acknowledgments

First, I would like to thank God for giving me the gift of music and language, without which none of this would be possible.

I wish to thank the following people for their contributions to my musical and personal development, education and other help in creating this book: my parents, for providing their children with a strong sense of our Korean heritage and cultural exposure from a young age; my music teachers, for fostering a love for music that has shaped my life thus far; and my wife and children, who are a constant inspiration to me.

In addition, thank you to Mrs. Choi, for your help in proofreading and translating; Yebin, for your amazing gift of song; Christina and Eric, for believing in me; and Cathy, for your tireless drive for perfection.

Published by Tuttle Publishing, an imprint of Periplus Editions (HK) Ltd.

www.tuttlepublishing.com

Copyright © 2014 Robert Sang-Ung Choi
Illustrations copyright © SamEe Back

Library of Congress Cataloging-in-Publication Data for this title is in progress

ISBN 978-0-8048-4468-0

Distributed by

North America, Latin America & Europe
Tuttle Publishing
364 Innovation Drive
North Clarendon, VT 05759-9436 U.S.A.
Tel: 1 (802) 773-8930
Fax: 1 (802) 773-6993
info@tuttlepublishing.com
www.tuttlepublishing.com

Japan
Tuttle Publishing
Yaekari Building, 3rd Floor
5-4-12 Osaki, Shinagawa-ku, Tokyo 141 0032
Tel: (81) 3 5437-0171
Fax: (81) 3 5437-0755
sales@tuttle.co.jp
www.tuttle.co.jp

Asia-Pacific
Berkeley Books Pte Ltd
61 Tai Seng Avenue, #02-12
Singapore 534167
Tel: (65) 6280 1330
Fax: (81) 6280 6290
inquiries@periplus.com.sg
www.periplus.com

First edition
17 16 15 14   6 5 4 3 2 1   1406EP

Printed in Hong Kong

Contents

Mountain Rabbit

Santokki 산토끼

Like many traditional songs "Mountain Rabbit" is testament to the love the Korean people have for their splendid natural heritage, particularly the beautiful mountains that are scattered through the land.

Sprightly ♩ = 72

1. 산 토 끼 토 끼 야 어 디 를 가 느 냐
San - tok - ki tok - ki - ya eo - di - reul ga - neun - ya?
Jack rab - bit, jack rab - bit, where are you go - ing?

2. 산 고 개 고 개 를 나 혼 자 넘 어 서
San - go - gae go - gae - reul na - hon - ja neo - meo - seo.
O - ver the moun - tain peaks, I'll climb them on my own.

깡 충 깡 충 뛰 면 서 어 디 를 가 느 냐
Ggang - chung ggang - chung dui - myeon - seo eo - di - reul ga - neun - ya?
Boun - cing as you're run - ning, where are you go - ing?

토 실 토 실 알 밤 을 주 워 서 올 테 야
To - shil to - shil al - bam - eul ju - weo - seo ol - te - ya.
Ripe and shi - ny chest - nuts, I'll find and bring them home.

Do the actions!

1. Place both hands on top of the head with index and middle fingers acting as bunny ears.
2. Next, place one hand at the forehead and look far into the distance, scanning left and right.
3. Hop like a bunny, with hands curled in front of the body like paws.
4. Again, place one hand at the forehead and look far into the distance, scanning left and right.
5. Walk, as though climbing a mountain, with one arm circular, as though holding a basket, and stop occasionally to pick up chestnuts and drop them into the basket.

Baby Calf
Songaji 송아지

Songs about animals and nature reflect the pride of the Korean people in their countryside. These topics are not reserved only for children's songs—even the Korean national anthem focuses on the beauty of the mountains and the national flower, *mugunghwa*, the hibiscus. "Baby Calf," with its simple lyrics and straight-forward melody is a favorite with younger children.

arr. Robert Sang-Ung Choi

Traditional

Moderately ♩ = 112

송아 - 지 송아 - 지 얼 룩 송아 지
Song - a - ji song - a - ji eol - luk song - a - ji.
Ba - by___ calf, ba - by___ calf, spot - ted ba - by calf.

5

엄 마 소 도 얼 룩 소 엄 마 - 닮 았 네
Eom - ma so - do eol - luk - so eom - ma dal - man - ne.
Mom - my cow is spot - ted too, and she looks just like you.

7

Clap, Clap, Clap!

Jjak jjak ggung 짝짜꿍

Composer Jung Soon Cheol was born in 1901 and came to be nicknamed Korea's Beethoven. He was also involved in the founding of the Children's Rights Movement—*Saekdonghwe*—in March 1923. He was abducted during the Korean War (1950–1952) and was never seen or heard from again, but his legacy lives on, both in his children's rights work and in his melodies, including this simple nursery song that Korean parents and grandparents sing to their children from a very young age. Hand clapping is a must!

arr. Robert Sang-Ung Choi

Jung Soon Cheol

Joyfully ♩= 132

엄 마 앞 에 서 짝 짜 꿍
Eom - ma ap - pe - seo jjak - jjak - ggung,
Clap for Mom - my___ clap, clap, clap,

아 빠 앞 에 서 짝 짜 꿍
ab - ba ap - pe - seo jjak - jjak-ggung.
clap for Dad - dy___ clap, clap, clap.

5

엄 마 한 숨 은 잠 자 고
Om - ma han - sum - eun jam - ja - go
Mom - my's wor - ries___ gone a - stray,

아 빠 주 름 살 펴 져 라
ab - ba ju - reum - sal pyeo- jeo - ra.
Dad - dy's wrin - kles___ fade a - way.

Splashing Around

Pong dang pong dang 퐁당 퐁당

Playfully written, this charming song celebrates the simple joys of being a child. Gestures commonly used while singing the song are throwing rocks into a stream, spreading arms wide, washing herbs, and tickling each other's hands.

arr. Robert Sang-Ung Choi

Traditional

Do the actions!

1. With the opening line of each verse, mime throwing stones into the stream.
2. Spread out your arms as wide as you can.
3. Mime washing the herbs in the river water.
4. With the last line of the song find a partner and tickle his or her hands!

10

Butterfly

Nabiya nabiya 나비야 나비야

Some Korean nursery rhymes are based on Western folk tunes, including this playful, catchy song, whose melody is borrowed from "Hänschen klein," the well-known German folk song.

arr. Robert Sang-Ung Choi

Traditional

Simply ♩ = 76

나 비 야 나 비 야 이 리 날 아 오 너 라
Na - bi - ya na - bi - ya i - ri na - ra o - neo - ra.
But - ter - fly, but - ter - fly, come on o - ver, fly to me.

노 랑 나 비 흰 나 비 춤 을 추 며 오 너 라
No - rang - na - bi huin - na - bi chum - eul - chu - myeo o - neo - ra.
Bright - ly col - ored but - ter - flies, danc - ing, danc - ing in the breeze.

Three Bears Song

Gom semari 곰 세마리

The Story of the Three Bears, known today as *Goldilocks and the Three Bears,* was originally published anonymously by Englishman Robert Southey in 1837. Since then, numerous composers from around the world have written songs based on the story. You can use any simple hand and body motions you like to accompany this song—the only requirement is to have fun!

arr. Robert Sang-Ung Choi

Traditional

Happily ♩ = 66

곰 세 마 리 가 한 집 에 있 어 아빠곰 엄마곰 애 기 곰
Gom se-ma-ri-ga han-ji-be-is-so ab-ba-gom eom-ma-gom ae-gi-gom.
Three bears, three bears, one hap-py fam'-ly, Dad-dy Bear, Mom-my Bear, Ba-by Bear.

아 빠 곰 은 뚱 뚱 해, 엄 마 곰 은 날 씬 해
Ab-ba-gom-eun ddung-ddung-hae eom-ma-gom-eun nal-shin-hae
Dad-dy Bear is big and fat, Mom-my Bear is beau-ti-ful,

애 기 곰 은 너 무 귀 여 워 으 쓱 으 쓱 잘 한 다
ae-gi-gom-eun neo-meo-gi-yeo-weo eu-sseuk eu-sseuk ja-rhan-da.
Ba-by Bear is real-ly real-ly cute, hap-py hap-py fam-i-ly.

15

Tadpole Song

Olchaengi song 올챙이송

This song describes the development of a tadpole into a frog, using fun-to-do actions and simple, short phrases that young children can easily learn.

arr. Robert Sang-Ung Choi

Traditional

Do the actions!

1. Put your hands on your hips and wriggle them from side to side.
2. Imagine your legs are the tadpole's hind legs and mime them breaking out of the egg.
3. Imagine your arms are the tadpole's forelegs and mime them breaking out of the egg.
4. Hop around like a frog!
5. Repeat the actions, following the lyrics.

Arirang 아리랑

This is Korea's most popular folk song and has been inscribed on the Representative List of the Intangible Cultural Heritage of Humanity by UNESCO. Every region of the country has its own unique version of the song; this one, sometimes called "Bonjo Arirang," is from central Korea and has become the unofficial second national anthem of the Republic of South Korea.

"Arirang represents all the joys and sorrows in the history and lives of Koreans. It is deeply rooted in Koreans' emotion as the cultural DNA."
—*National Folk Museum of Korea*

Thinking of Older Brother

Obba saenggak 오빠 생각

During the Japanese occupation of Korea (1910–1945), eleven-year-old Choi Sun Ae's brother went to Seoul to buy shoes and never returned, inspiring her to write these lyrics. The cheerful music—written by Park Tae Jun—may seem like a strange contrast to the sad words, but during the occupation the Japanese prohibited songs that were negative or depressing in nature. Having a relatively "happy" melody was a way of masking mournful sentiments.

arr. Robert Sang-Ung Choi

Choi Sun Ae
Park Tae Jun

With deep sentiment ♩. = 42

1. 뜸 북 뜸 북 뜸 북 새   논 – 에 서 울 고
Ddeum - buk ddeum - buk ddeum - buk - sae   non - ae - seo   ul - go.
Birds   are   cry - ing   in   the   fields,   cry - ing   in   the   fields.

2. 기 럭 기 럭 기 러 기   북 – 에 서 오 고
Gi - reok gi - reok gi - reo - gi   bug - ae - seo   o - go.
Geese   are   com - ing   from   the   north,   com - ing   from   the   north.

뻐 꾹 뻐 꾹 뻐 – 꾹 새   숲 에 서 – 울 제
Bbeo - gguk bbeo - gguk bbeo - gguk - sae   sup - ae - seo - ul - je.
Cuck - oos   call - ing   from__   the   woods,   call - ing   from__   the   woods.

귀 뜰 귀 뜰 귀 뚜 라 미   슬 피 울 – 건 만
Gui - ddeul gui - ddeul gui-du - ra - mi   seul - pi ul - geon-man.
Crick - ets   sing   a   bit - ter   song,   bit - ter   mel - o - dy.

20

Boat Song

Baetnorae 뱃노래

Korea's fishing culture has deep roots, and this song, in which fishermen celebrate their daily life on the open sea, expresses a sense of pride in the fishing tradition. There are several versions of "Boat Song," all based upon a set of interchangeable verses—those included here are two of the most popular. Traditionally "Boat Song" is immediately followed by the more upbeat "Fast Boat Song" (page 24-25).

arr. Robert Sang-Ung Choi

Traditional

Flowingly ♩ = 132

어 기 야 디 여 — 차   어 야
Eo - gi - ya di - yeo - cha   eo - ya-
Eo - gi - ya di - yeo - cha   eo - ya-

디 야 — 어 기 — 여 차 — — 뱃 놀 이 가 — — 잔
di - ya - eo - gi - yeo - cha baet - no - ri ga - jan-
di - ya - eo - gi - yeo - cha, the__ bount - i - ful o - ceans

다   1. 부 딪 치 는 파 도 —
da.   Bu - dit - chi - neun pa - do -
call.   *Surg - ing, splash - ing, waves are a*

     2. 만 경 — — 창 —
     Man - gyeong - - chang - -
     Soar - ing,_____ sea - gulls a

22

Fast Boat Song

Jajin baetnorae 자진 뱃노래

Action songs are not just for children! In performances of this song, which expresses the joy of fishermen as they bring in their catch, Korean folk groups use simple hand gestures to illustrate the laying and bringing in of the nets.

arr. Robert Sang-Ung Choi

Traditional

Mother, Sister

Eommaya nunaya 엄마야 누나야

This song is an arrangement of a poem by Kim So Weol—known as the "folk-song poet"—written during the Japanese occupation of Korea (1910–1945). In this haunting piece, a child longs for carefree days and freedom from oppression.

Kim So Weol
Ahn Seong Hyeon

Blue Birds

Saeya saeya 새야 새야

"Blue Birds" was inspired by events that led to the Donghak Peasant Revolt of 1894, when farmers rebelled against many years of exploitation by rich and unscrupulous landowners. Although the lyrics appear on the surface to have a childlike simplicity and calm, the underlying tension and fear are palpable.

arr. Robert Sang-Ung Choi

Traditional

Doraji 도라지

Doraji is the Korean word for Chinese bellflower, a plant that is found in mountainous areas of Asia and whose root is known for its medicinal properties. In Korea the root is also eaten in salads and soups. There are many versions of the lyrics of this popular song; those selected here are the most widely known.

arr. Robert Sang-Ung Choi

Traditional

Gently lilting ♩. = 72

도 라 지 도 — 라 지 백 — 도 라 — — 지
Do - ra - ji do - ra - ji baek - do - ra - ji
Bell - flow - er, bell - flow - er, white bell - flow - er,

한 두 — 뿌 리 — 만 캐 — 어 도 — — —
Han du___ bbu - ri - man kae - yeo do___
Pick on - ly one___ or two roots and___ still___

CD Track Listings

The Tuttle Story "Books to Span the East and West"

Many people are surprised to learn that the world's largest publisher of books on Asia had its humble beginnings in the tiny American state of Vermont. The company's founder, Charles E. Tuttle, belonged to a New England family steeped in publishing.

Immediately after WW II, Tuttle served in Tokyo under General Douglas MacArthur and was tasked with reviving the Japanese publishing industry. He later founded the Charles E. Tuttle Publishing Company, which thrives today as one of the world's leading independent publishers.

Though a westerner, Tuttle was hugely instrumental in bringing a knowledge of Japan and Asia to a world hungry for information about the East. By the time of his death in 1993, Tuttle had published over 6,000 books on Asian culture, history and art—a legacy honored by the Japanese emperor with the "Order of the Sacred Treasure," the highest tribute Japan can bestow upon a non-Japanese.

With a backlist of 1,500 titles, Tuttle Publishing is more active today than at any time in its past—inspired by Charles Tuttle's core mission to publish fine books to span the East and West and provide a greater understanding of each.